GURU NANAK
THE FOUNDER OF SIKHISM

Contents

Guru is Born	5
Childhood and Education	8
Miracles	14
Worldly Affairs	22
Divine Call	30
Divine Work Begins	32
Preaching the Gospel of God	39
Panja Sahib Gurudwara	62
Cup of Milk	64
Reforming the High and Mighty	67
Sikander Lodi	68
Hamza Gaus	70
Kauda the Cannibal	73
Guru in Baghdad	74
Babar's Invasion	76
Back Home	78
Bhai Budha	80
Rise of the Second Guru	84
Attaining Samadhi	88
Glossary	92

Guru is Born

Born on 15 April 1469 at Talwandi in the Sheikupura district which is now a part of West Pakistan, Nanak was the founder of Sikhism. He was born to Mata Tripta Devi and Mehta Kalian Das. His father, also known as Mehta Kalu, was a *bedi* patwari. Kalu Mehta called for the family astrologer, Pandit Hardyal, to draw up the baby's *janampatri*.

When the *janampatri* was drawn, Pandit Hardyal was very happy and he pleaded with Mehta Kalu to let him have a glimpse of the baby. After touching the feet of the infant he told the parents that they were fortunate to have a son like him, who had a very bright future and would rule over the people of the world by his supreme grace.

"He will be a great person and glorious as well and will be known throughout the world for his divine teachings," he added. The little baby was going to be a unique king of kings.

The parents were overjoyed to hear the predictions. He later established the Sikh religion and is known throughout the world as Guru Nanak.

The child was named 'Nanak' after his sister, Bibi Nanaki. Nanaki was Nanak's confidante, a person from whom he received the greatest understanding and affection, and who saw something extraordinary in Nanak.

The people who came to visit him were amazed to see a smiling child. Everyone was drawn to him by his soft, compassionate and humane eyes. The people admitted that there was a certain peace and calm on his face that attracted them. Baby Nanak had already begun his work of ruling over the hearts of people, and spreading the message of peace and compassion among others.

Childhood and Education

Nanak led a very simple childhood like that of other children of his age. But unlike other children, he did not spend his time and energy on childish pursuits. His friends loved him and enjoyed his company because he was friendly and always ready to help when they needed him. He was always ready to help poor and the deprived.

Nanak was very kind-hearted and generous. He would willingly give away all that he had to anyone who seemed to need it. He always loved to meet holy men like the *fakirs* and monks.

At a tender age of five years, Nanak is said to have voiced interest in divine subjects. When Nanak was seven years old, he was sent to school to learn language and airthmetic under Pandit Gopal. Unlike the other children, the bright Nanak picked up the subjects in a shortwhile.

One day, Pandit Gopal found Nanak sitting apart from other boys and writing something on a wooden tablet. He got curious and wanted to know what the boy was busy doing.

"Show me your wooden tablet Nanak. I want to see what have you written," he said.

However, when Nanak went up with his *patti*, the teacher was more than amazed. Before him was a poem, written in acrostics (in which the lines follow alphabetical order).When Pandit Gopalji went through the content of the poem, he was completely amazed. It was based on the subject of God, universe and man, on man's duty towards God and towards his fellow-beings.

The pandit took the child to his father and told him, "Your son is no ordinary man, but an *avatar* who is destined to be a teacher of mankind."

When Mehta Kalu insisted on higher education, the teacher humbly replied that the child knew enough to teach his own teachers. He bowed before Nanak and took his leave.

So Nanak stopped going to Pandit Gopal's school. But Mehta Kalu was not satisfied with Nanak's education. He felt very uneasy seeing his young son spending his free time in the company of *sadhus* and *fakirs*. Once again the family astrologer Pandit Hardyal guidance for his son was sought.

Pandit Hardyal was well aware of Nanak's religious inclination.

"Mehta Kalu, you send Nanak to a Sankrit scholar to learn Sanskrit, where he can also study the vedas and *shastras* which are the subjects closest to his heart," he said.

Mehta Kalu readily agreed to the suggestion and accordingly, Nanak was sent to a Sanskrit scholar named Brijnath.

Here too, the child quietly learned all that his teacher had to offer and resumed his old ways of associating freely with the wandering ascetics in the forests and meditating at home.

Mehta Kalu, of course, was disturbed. Like all fathers, he also wanted his son to be a successful man. But he could see no signs of it in Nanak. He then decided to consult Rai Bular, who was the *zamindar* of the village, regarding his son's future. Now, Rai Bular had often watched Nanak engaged in divine meditation, and had come to love and cherish him.

"You send your son to learn Persian," Rai Bular said.

"Since Persian is the language in which all the state documents and accounts are written, I can give Nanak the charge of the office on completion of his studies," he futher added.

Nanak's father was very pleased at the suggestion, and immediately sent his son to a *madrasah*. His teacher was *Maulvi* Qutab-ud-in who taught him Persian and Arabic. Hence too the teacher felt that he, had imparted all that he knew and Nanak seemed to know more than him. Nanak stopped going to the *madrasah*, and once again began to seek the company of religious men who were his elders in age, and peers in knowledge.

Miracles

When Nanak reached the age of thirteen, he had to undergo the *yagyopavita* ceremony in which *janeu* was placed around the neck. Pandit Hardyal was invited to perform the ceremony. But young Nanak refused to wear it. Everyone present in the ceremony was surprised and stunned.

"It is an ancient custom in which the thread woven of seven cotton strings is worn around the neck that symbolises the spiritual birth of a Hindu," explained the *Pandit*.

But Nanak was adamant.

He argued and refused to proceed with the ceremony.

"I can never wear something that my pure soul cannot take along with it, and will instead, break, get soiled or be burnt," Nanak said.

He said, "I want a thread made of truth, purity and virtues of day-to-day life. If all these things do not come with wearing this thread I will never wear it."

The strong words of the thirteen year old boy silenced the assembled guests in wonder.

Seeing the adolescent Nanak's disinterest in the matters of the world, wealth and fame, his father decided to engage him in a grazier's job. He felt that tending the cattle he would learn to be responsible and thereby pick up the ways of the world.

He told his son, "You will take our cattle for grazing to the forest". Nanak agreed happily. Every morning he set out with the cattle, and while they grazed he meditated under a tree, and returned home with them in the evening.

One day when Nanak was deep in meditation, the cattle tramped into the nearby field of a peasant and ate up the crops. When the peasant saw his crops being destroyed, he screamed at Nanak.

"Your cattle have destroyed my fields and you will have to pay for it," The owner was angry and furious and rushed to report it to the *zamindar* of the village, Rai Bular.

Nanak was ordered to pay for the loss.

Nanak calmly replied, "I will pay you for the loss if there has been any loss actually."

Hearing this, all those who were present there went up to the fields. The peasant was baffled to see the unharmed field of crops. The confused peasant was embarrassed and humbly asked for Nanak's forgiveness.

Another day, in the peak of summer, Nanak lay under a tree while his cattle grazed. Just then Rai Bular happened to pass by. He was amazed at what he saw. Before him lay Nanak, and a cobra sat near him, shielding him from the sunlight with its hood. Before he could wake Nanak up, the snake quietly slithered away.

Rai Bular came up to him and Nanak smiled. He quietly bowed down before Nanak, in great respect. He knew that he was standing before the messenger of God.

Nanak began devoting most of his time to the worship of God. There were times when he would even forget to eat his meals. Seeing his condition Mehta Kalu thought he was ill, and quickly summoned a physician. However, when Nanak was being examined, he shocked the physician by his melodious voice and words.

He said to the physician, "This illness is given to me by Lord Almighty and only He can cure it."

It was only then the physician realised that this extraordinary boy had no mortal sickness.

Then one day, Nanak happened to meet a beggar who was being treated with utter contempt by everyone. Nanak could not tolerate such an attitude and he asked the beggar to beg God alone for his needs and not men.

The poor beggar could not grasp the meaning of such divine words and Nanak, realising his plight, gave his clothes to him and went home. When rebuked by his mother for this act, he coolly replied that he had received divine orders for giving them away to a needy person.

Worldly Affairs

Nanak's way of life started to worry his father who decided to teach him to earn money, hoping that it would change his ways of leading a life of that of a recluse.

"You take these twenty-one silver coins and purchase some material from the *mandi* in Chuharkana to start some business," Nanak's father said.

He was accompanied by Bala, a friend, on this trip.

While on his way to the mandi, he reached a place where many saints were staying. Nanak immediately paid his respects to them, and on finding that these *sadhus* had not eaten anything for many days, he arranged for their food with whatever money he had.

They bought flour, pulses, rice and *ghee* from the *mandi* and Nanak fed the holy men with true devotion. He was never so satisfied as at that moment, when he was serving God's men. For him this was the best and the most profitable bargain.

Incidentally, there is a gurudwara called *Sachcha Sauda* or good bargain at the very site where he had fed the saints.

Nanak's parents, however, were very disappointed with this act of his. To end their distress, they decided to get him married and make him worldly wise. Nanak was sixteen years old when he got married to Mata Sulakhani, daughter of Baba Mul Chand of Batala. Sulakhni was a gentle and virtuous bride who built a very happy and hospitable home.

In the meantime Nanak's sister, Nanaki, and her husband Jairam invited him to Sultanpur. On the advice of Rai Bular, Mehta Kalu sent Nanak to Sultanpur. Rai Bular wrote to Daulat Khan, the Governor of Sultanpur, recommending Nanak in glorious terms. After reading the letter and at the request of his brother-in-law, who was a high official in the Sultanpur State Services, Nanak was appointed as the store incharge. This made his parents and wife very happy. In course of time, two sons were born to Nanak, Baba Siri Chand in August 1494, and Baba Lakhmi Das in March 1497. While Siri Chand was inclined towards spiritual matters and lived the life of an ascetic, the younger son, Lakhmi Das, married and raised a family.

Around this time, Nanak's childhood friend, Bhai Mardana, also came to live with him. They were very close to each other. Whenever Nanak sat down to sing hymns in praise of God, Mardana would play the *rabab* so sweetly that listeners gathered around them were enchanted with the depth and devotion in the songs.

Though Nanak became a householder he did not neglect his religious duties. He often used to donate free grains to the poor, though by the grace of God nothing ever fell short.

But there were a few jealous men who did not like the popularity and esteem enjoyed by Nanak.

They went to the *nawab* to poison his ears that Nanak was misusing the granary.

"*Nawab Sahab*, there will be nothing left in the granary one day," one of the workers said.

Nawab Daulat Khan fell prey to their vicious reports and went to the store himself to inspect it. But when the provisions were checked they were found to be not only sufficient, but a little more than expected. The *Nawab's* respect for Nanak grew from that day.

Divine Call

Nanak spent twelve years as a family man, faithfully attending to all the duties.

It was now time to move onto his mission in life and answer the divine call.

One day, early in the morning, as usual, he went to the river for his bath. He plunged into the river and sat in meditation under the water. His friend Mardana sat on the bank waiting for him. People started to cry as they were fraught with the fear that he had drowned in the river. It was only after three days had passed that Nanak returned to the other side of the river. The village was overjoyed to see him back. Soon he disclosed the secret of his disappearance.

Nanak then explained that he had gone to a lonely spot in the forest, on the other side of the river, where he received his orders from God regarding his work.

Divine Work Begins

Next day, Nanak began meditating by the riverside. He did not talk to anyone throughout the day and night. Finally he began speaking. The first words he uttered were, "There is no Hindu, no Mussalman."

Slowly people began gathering around him and Nanak preached them. The more the people realised that he was sent for their good, to guide them from darkness to light, the louder they sang his praises. It was from this day that Nanak was called 'Guru Nanak.'

Guru Nanak preached that all Hindus and Mussalmans were followers of the same God. This spread like wild fire and was soon heard by a few fanatic Muslims. They complained to the *qazi* in the *nawab's* court about it. The *qazi* quickly informed the *nawab* that Nanak was spreading crude and disrespectful messages among the people.

The *nawab*, however, was an admirer of the Guru. He invited Nanak to his court and respectfully gave him a seat next to himself.

The *qazi* asked Guru Nanak, "You say that there is no Hindu, no Mussalman; then to which religion do you belong?"

"I am neither a Hindu nor a Muslim, but a lover of God and a servant of man," replied Nanak. "All religions are different paths leading to one God and His abode," he further added.

He also said that all Hindus and Muslims are children of the same father, and thus, are brothers, and they should live together like members of the same family.

While they were discussing the matter, it was time for the *namaz*.

The *nawab* said, "You must join us in prayers if you are not a Hindu."

Nanak willingly said yes to this request. But when all the Muslims knelt down, Nanak kept standing. The *qazi* was furious and asked the *nawab* to punish Nanak severely for not taking their prayers seriously.

At this, the *nawab* asked Guru Nanak, "Why didn't you joined us in our prayers after you agreed to do so?"

Nanak answered politely, "I was the only one who was truly saying the prayers because my thoughts were not rambling like yours."

He further said that the *qazi* was only physically present during the prayers, while his mind was busy thinking of the mare who had just delivered a foal, as he was afraid that it might fall into the well in the courtyard. As for the *nawab sahib*, he too was thinking about his agents who were busy buying and selling horses in Kabul.

On hearing this, the heads of all men present hung with shame because Guru Nanak had correctly read their minds. The Guru then explained that all those people who do not say their prayers in true devotion to God are not praying at all. The words are meanigless. Saying this, he departed.

Preaching the Gospel of God

After this incident at Sultanpur, Nanak began to spread his word as a teacher of the world. He decided to take this giant mission and went on long journeys called *udasis*. But before that, he wanted to go to Talwandi and inform his parents of his intended tours. He travelled from village to village conveying his message to people. He established *manjis* in all the places that he visited on the way. In every place he stopped, he taught people how to live and act as the children of God. He sang to them his sacred songs and explained his views to them.

When he reached Talwandi, his parents were shocked to see their son dressed as a *sadhu*. They pleaded him to cast away those clothes and support them in their old age by living with them and doing his duties as a son. But Nanak explained to them that he had to obey God's call.

"I have to go now to teach the path of love to people all over the world and serve the poor, suffering and needy," said Nanak.

He bid farewell to his tearful parents and set out on *udasi* towards the east. He wanted to visit the holy places of the Hindus after having renounced his home.

After leaving his home he began roaming everywhere, preaching the message of God to people. He was accompanied by his friend and disciple, Bhai Mardana. Guru Nanak used to give sermons, chant God's name with Bhai Mardana on the *rabab* and slowly their followers numbered in thousands.

He would often do something that was unconventional aiming to attract the attention of a large group of people. People often took such actions as an insult to their religion, which drew the angry pilgrims around him. Once he had the defiant crowd surrounding him, then he would proceed to tell them their errors and convert them to his point of view, which was the right way to worship and please God.

He wore *jutti* instead of a '*khadaun*'. He had a mark on his forehead in the style of the Hindus, and on his head he wore a conical cap of Muslim *qalandars*. This indicated his desire to find a new religion based on Hindus and Muslims, the principles of both which would be acceptable to both.

One day, Guru Nanak came to know that a Hindu religious fair was to be held at Kurukshetra on the occasion of a solar eclipse. Thousands of people were to take a dip in the sacred tank that day. He immediately decided to visit that place with the object of preaching to the gathered pilgrims.

On reaching there, he took his seat near the tank and began singing one of his hymns. However, not many people paid attention to his singing, since they were all too busy washing their sins and praying to the Sun God.

Around that time, a queen and her son came along to the fair. The young prince, who had killed a deer while hunting in the neighbouring forest presented his kill to the Guru. Nanak accepted it before the outrageous pilgrims who ran to beat him up.

Thus the Guru successfully attracted all the attention of the crowd which led to an apportunity for his sermon.

After his short stay in Kurukshetra, the Guru resumed his tour. He halted for a day or two at every village and preached his religion to the people there.

One morning, while he was bathing in the river Ganga he found people offering handfuls of water to the sun to relieve the spirits of their departed ancestors.

Nanak asked a *brahmin*, "Does this water actually reach the dead ancestors". When the *brahmin* emphatically said it would, Guru Nanak began throwing water in the opposite direction. On seeing this, one of the priests present there objected to it.

"You should not do this as this is against the religion," said the priest.

"I am sending water to my fields in Punjab, which is even nearer than the abode of my ancestors," replied Nanak.

The people present there realised what the Guru was trying to say and felt that he was indeed right. They requested him to give them some good advice and guidance. Guru Nanak then asked them to live their lives as good, honest, truthful lives and to be god-fearing besides sharing their belongings with others.

He told them that the best way to have anything reach their ancestors is by giving to the poor and the needy, in the name of those ancestors. The people present there willingly became his disciples and vowed to live and act as advised by the Guru.

The Guru took his seat and then began to talk about their false beliefs on meat eating.

"Though you all protest against eating meat but you all do the same by sucking blood of innocent people with your cruel and unjust deeds, by snatching or stealing other people's rights and belongings," said Nanak.

He also explained to them that a solar eclipse was a natural phenomenon and no demon had anything to do with it..

"By working hard you can earn your living and by sharing your earnings with the poor and needy, you can win the approval of God Almighty," said Guru Nanak.

When the gathered pilgrims heard all this, it had a strange effect on them. All those who had come to beat him, became his disciples. They established a *dharamshala* there to provide food and shelter for to the poor and the weary, and to sing hymns in the praise of God.

While travelling, Guruji reached a village called Amanabad along with Bhai Mardana. He was welcomed with great respect and love by the people of the village. In that village lived one of Nanak's disciples named Bhai Lalo. On hearing the news of Nanak's arrival, he went to invite him for a meal.

"Guruji I live in a very small cottage nearby. My family and I would be highly obliged if you allow us to serve you," said the carpenter.

Guru Nanak was moved by his humble words and he immediately agreed to stay with them. "The warmth of your heart has charmed me. I'll be very happy and delighted to saty with you in your cottage," replied Guru Nanak.

He happily ate whatever was offered to him. He never made any distinction among men. To him, all men were equal and were children of God.

In the same village lived Malik Bhago, who was the manager. He was a greedy, cruel and corrupt man. One day, he arranged a *brahm-bhoj* and invited all the religious and holy men of the village. He also wanted to invite Guru Nanak to the feast.

"I want Nanak to be the part of our feast. You go and invite Nanak to our special feast," told Malik Bhago to his servant.

The servant went to obey the orders of his master but came back disappointed.

"Guruji has refused the invitation of attending the *brahm-bhoj*," said the servant.

On hearing this Malik Bhago was very angry and went to Guru Nanak to ask for an explanation.

"Guruji I invited you to such a grand feast where you could have eaten much better food than these dried chapatis," said Bhago arrogantly.

"Go and bring some food from your home," told Guruji to Malik Bhago.

Then taking the latter's *chapatis* in his right hand and the rich food of Malik Bhago's in his left, he squeezed the two. All the people present there were shocked to see drops of blood coming out of Malik Bhago's food and drops of milk from Bhai Lalo's *rotis*.

"Your food is made from money that you have earned by torturing and exploiting the poor and weak, while Bhai Lalo's food is made from hard-earned money that he happily shares with others. This is the reason why your food is dripping blood and Lalo's food is dripping milk," told Guruji to completely ashamed Malik Bhago.

He advised Malik Bhago to earn money by hard work and to serve the needy with a true heart. The guilty man fell at the Guru's feet, and asked forgiveness.

In course of his travels, Guru Nanak reached Lahore. There he sat on the banks of the river Ravi and began singing sacred songs with Bhai Mardana on the *rabab*. Slowly a crowd gathered to hear him sing and preach. Among the listeners was a rich man called Duni Chand.

Duni Chand went to invite Guru Nanak to bless his house on the occasion of the *shradh* ceremony of his father.

"Guruji, I am your devotee and would feel blessed if you accept my invitation for lunch," said Duni Chand.

Nanak happily agreed and went along with him to his house.

Dhuni Chand's wealth had blinded him and he had become arrogant. He never helped the under privileged. After having lunch, Guruji called Duni Chand to sit by his side. ,

"Take this needle and keep it safe with you," said Nanak. Duni Chand was very confused and could not understand the meaning of this gesture.

"Guruji, why are you giving me this needle," asked puzzled Duni Chand.

"I want you to bring this needle along with you because I'll ask for it back in the next world."

An already confused Duni Chand could not grasp the meaning of this action and took it to his wife. The pious woman understood and explained to Duni Chand that Nanak meant to show him that a man can carry nothing with him, not even a needle, to the next world. Duni Chand was suddenly enlightened. He felt ashamed of himself and pleaded forgiveness from Guruji.

"From now onwards I'll help the unfortunate people," said Duni Chand.

After his short stay at Lahore, Guru Nanak reached Batala, and choosing a particular spot prepared himself to work for his mission. The owner of that area, Karorimal, did not approve of someone occupying his land. He decided to turn Guru Nanak away. No sooner he had started from his house his horse stumbled, and Karorimal had to return, hurt.

After a few days, he set out again, his eyesight was afflicted. A shocked Karorimal was then told by his men that his evil motive to drive a holy man away had caused him the pain. The third time, Karorimal decided to pay his respects to Guru Nanak, but as he proceeded he was blinded again. Then finally, he decided to walk all the way and this time he reached Guru Nanak safely. He found him surrounded by devotees, singing hymns. He fell at the Guru's feet and pleaded forgiveness.

"Guruji, please grant me permission to dedicate my life to the service of God and allow me to serve you," requested Karorimal.

Guru Nanak blessed him and proposed to call the village 'Kartarpur' which meant 'the seat of God, the Creator.' Soon the village became the seat of Guru Nanak and all his disciples. It was here that Guru Nanak started ploughing a piece of land and taught the people that each man should live on one's own labour and produce.

Guru Nanak also travelled to Baghdad, which was a powerful centre of Islam. So much so, that the mere presence of a non believer of the faith there could be taken as a blot on Islam. Guru Nanak was aware of this attitude, but he was not at all afraid. On arriving there, he chose a graveyard for his stay. Early next morning, he asked Bhai Mardana to play the *rabab*, while he sang a sacred song.

In that centre of Islam, music had never been heard before, as it was forbidden. Everyone there was amazed and flocked to see that who had the courage to break the law in that city. He then began to recite the *Japji* to the people gathered around him. He spoke of the millions of upper and lower regions that existed in the universe.

Soon the *pir* or the religious head of the place was informed about the Guru. He ordered the offender to be brought in his presence immediately.

"Go get that culprit and bring him here," ordered the *pir* to one of the servants.

But Guru Nanak refused to obey, and asked the *pir* to come to him and hear him sing. The *pir* was furious and he ordered his men to stone the culprit to death. But as the

angry crowd moved forward, they heard the soothing words sung by the Guru and his disciples, all their anger seemed to vanish. They threw away the stones and heard him sing of God's greatness and glory with great attention.

When the *pir* heard this he decided to see the Guru. He took his young son with him to the graveyard to see him.

"Who are you and why are you acting against the law of Islam," asked the angry *pir*.

"I've done nothing to hurt the spirit of Islam," replied Guruji calmly.

The *pir* again questioned Guru Nanak and asked him to prove his words.

"Prove that there are innumerable upper and lower regions as you said," said the vexed *pir*.

Guru Nanak explained, "If your heart and mind are pure and your thoughts and feelings are fixed on the Supreme Lord, you can see the various regions."

Hearing this, the young son of the *pir* expressed a wish to see the various regions.

Guru Nanak then gently held his hand and said, "Dear son just think of God alone with pure heart and mind."

The boy did as asked by Guruji and felt himself soaring high at great speed to limitless space. He was convinced of the Guru's words. After a while he opened his eyes and found himself in the graveyard next to his father. The *pir* saw a changed look on his son's face which told him that what the boy believed was true indeed. He fell at the Guru's feet and asked forgiveness. All those present there also bowed before the Guru and he blessed them all.

On the spot, where the Guru sat at Baghdad, a platform was later erected by one of the Guru's disciples. On the wall behind it is an inscription in a language which is a mixture of Arabic, Persian and Turkish, in the memory of his visit.

Panja Sahib Gurudwara

One interesting incident occurred when Guru Nanak reached Hasan Abdul, now in Pakistan. There was a Muslim *fakir* named Baba Hasan Abdul Wali Qandhari who owned a house by the side of a fresh water spring, the water from which flowed into a tank and from there to the plains below.

When Qandhari heard of Guru Nanak, he was filled with jealousy and so he stopped the water supply to punish the people who spoke so highly of the Guru. The people begged Nanak to do something. "Guruji the water supply has been stopped. Please help us with your divine powers," requested the villagers. Guru Nanak lifted a small stone nearby and water began to flow from there. All the people rejoiced and were very happy. But Qandhari was very angry and he rolled down a big stone on Guru Nanak. This, however, was stopped by his hand. An imprint of Guru's open hand or *panja* was made on the stone.

It exists to this day and is called as *Panja Sahib* or the Holy Hand-print. Qandhari was awestruck on seeing this and he bowed at the Guru's feet, begging forgiveness. This holy and revered place was named *Panja Sahib*.

Cup of Milk

Guru Nanak, on reaching Multan, heard that some Muslim *fakirs* were exploiting the poor and ignorant people in the name of religion. He began spreading his message there.

Soon people began to have faith in God once again. The native *fakirs* were very angry and decided to drive him away. To convey this, they sent him a cup of milk full to the brim, symbolising that the place was full of religious men already and there was no need of him. Guru Nanak put inside the cup some *batashas* and a jasmine flower over it and sent it back.

"When a bowl of milk is sent as a gift it should not be returned," told Mardana to his master.

Guru Nanak replied, "They have not sent this milk for my use. The have sent me the message that Multan is already full of *pirs* and there is no room for any other *guru*."

"The *batashas* and the jasmine in the milk convey that there is always a special place for me and that I am here to spread the Lord's message of love, peace and devotion," said Guruji.

The proud and arrogant *pirs* realized their mistake and asked Guruji's forgiveness.

"Pardon us ,O revered Guru! We were self-conceited. Kindly bless us," pleaded the *pirs*.

Guru Nanak blessed them and went on with his further journey.

Reforming the High and Mighty

While staying in Multan, Guru Nanak and Bhai Mardana arrived at a place called Tulamba. Around this place lived a notorious robber named Sajjan, who used to welcome travellers in his *serai*, treat them generously and then kill them after robbing them of their wealth. Guru Nanak heard of his cruelty and ill ways and decided to teach him a lesson.

Guru Nanak and his companions stopped at the *serai*. They appeared to be very rich to Sajjan and his men. At night, Guru Nanak began singing songs about the evil deeds of criminals who betrayed the trust of people to fulfill their selfish desires, while Mardana played the *rabab*. Sajjan heard them singing the compositons and accurately felt that Guru Nanak knew everything about him and his character.

Sajjan was completely taken aback at Guru Nanak's insight. He felt ashamed and guilty and flung himself at the Guru's feet asking forgiveness. Guru Nanak advised him to distribute all his wealth amongst the poor people and to live like an honest man. He asked Sajjan to live up to his name which means a true gentleman and a good human being. Sajjan thanked him and made a *dharamshala*, which was the first Sikh gurudwara established by the Guru.

Sikander Lodi

In the course of his travels, Guru Nanak reached Delhi. Sikander Lodi, the emperor at that time was a cruel man who used to oppress his subjects. He wanted everyone to turn to Islam and eradicate all other religions.

"I order you all to convert to Islam and be a true muslim, and anyone who does not follow this will have to choose between Islam and death," said Lodi.

All religious people were tortured and brutally treated in his rule, and Guru Nanak and Mardana were also arrested and put in prison.

Guru Nanak was dismayed at the sight of the terrible condition of the imprisoned innocent religious people. He began singing a song in his intense and heart-rending voice. All the listeners, including the jailers and the emperor, were delighted and filled with ecstasy by the songs on the supreme Lord and His mercy. He sang of the omniscient Lord who saw everything and paid likewise. Sikander Lodi was so touched by the song that he realized his wrong doings. He freed all the prisoners and begged forgiveness from Guru Nanak. After that Sikander Lodi ruled wisely, always keeping the Guru's advice in mind.

Hamza Gaus

Travelling further westwards, Guru Nanak stopped at Sialkot where he was called to solve a local problem. There was a Muslim *fakir* called Hamza Gaus to whom a Hindu *Khatri* had come asking for a son as he was childless. He promised to offer his first son in the *fakir's* service, if he got more than one son.

Three sons were born to him and he asked Hamza Gaus to let him buy his child back. The *fakir* refused, threatening to destroy the whole city and its inhabitants if the Hindu did not abide by his promise. The *fakir* had entered the dome for a forty day meditation to destroy the city.

Guru Nanak and Mardana went to the place where *fakir* had locked himself and sang songs outside the dome. On hearing the music, he broke his meditation and came out very angry.

"You should not punish the innocent people for the sin of one wrongdoer," emphasised Guruji. "They are all alike and don't believe in keeping their words and hence should be destroyed," claimed the angry *fakir*.

The Guru decided to reveal the truth to him. He gave some money to Mardana and asked him to purchase a packet each of 'truth' and 'false hood'. He went to the city and moved from shop to shop but all in vain. Finally, Moola, the shopkeeper, took the coins from him and wrote the answer in writing. On one slip, he wrote 'Life is a falsehood' and on the other he wrote 'Death is the truth.'

The Guru showed this to *fakir* and he understood that there are some people who do not deserve to die.

Guru Nanak told him that it was wrong to punish the whole city for one person. And no man should and can destroy another, if he is really a devotee of God. Hamza Gaus realised his mistake and went on to preach the gospel of Guru Nanak to men.

Kauda the Cannibal

Guru Nanak was still on his travels and going towards the Deccan. At one place, Guruji was alarmed to hear cries of agony calling out for help. In a jungle nearby, there lived a tribe called Bheels, known for their barbarous nature. It was said that they would kill and eat anyone passing through that stretch. Kauda was their chief.

When Guruji came to know about it, he decided to end this barbaric act. Guruji directly went to the place where the Kauda was residing. When Kauda saw him approaching he was very happy and started to heat the huge cauldron of oil to cook the visitors. But he found that the oil would not heat at all. No doubt the fire burned, but it had lost the power to heat the oil.

Stupefied, Kauda began to tremble as he could not understand what was wrong. He gripped Guru Nanak by his arm and made him sit in the cauldron. Guruji sat in it and remained unharmed.

On seeing this miraculous spectacle, enlightenment dawned over Kauda. And he fell on his knees and began to cry.

The Guru said, "You decide your destiny by your actions, so always be humble."

"You have become blind with arrogance and do not know what you are doing. But you have to change yourself," Guruji said calmly.

"You are also a child of God. You must earn an honest living and share with others," he further added.

Kauda was overwhelmed by the Guru's words of solace and changed his ways overnight. Guru Nanak had succeeded in reforming a cannibal into a loyal friend and servant.

Guru in Baghdad

Spreading the message of love, peace and brotherhood, Guru Nanak reached Baghdad. Khalifa, who was the ruler of Baghdad, was a tyrant man and notorious for looting his subjects and exploiting them.

Guru Nanak set out for the place and reaching the main road, he began to pile up a big heap of pebbles and stones. After a while, the Khalifa's pageant passed by and seeing Guru Nanak collecting pebbles, the Khalifa stopped to enquire.

"Why are you collecting these pebbles and making heaps of them," asked surprised Khalifa.

Guru Nanak calmly replied "I am going to carry all this with me when I die."

When the Khalifa expressed surprise at this folly, Guru Nanak replied that if the king was going to take all his wealth with him, he could also take his pebbles. The Khalifa understood the insight of what the Guru was trying to explain by this example.

"All that a man needs is some clothes to cover himself and some bread to survive. Everything else can be used to help the poor and needy," told Guru Nanak.

The transformed Khalifa soon distributed his wealth amongst his people and respectfully presented a robe to Guru Nanak with *Aayats* of the Holy Quran inscribed on it. The robe is still preserved in the gurudwara at Dera Baba Nanak.

Babar's Invasion

It was in the year 1521 A.D. that Guru Nanak's prophecy of Babar's invasion of India came true. Guru Nanak immediately reached Saidpur and was terribly shaken when he saw the plight of the city and its inhabitants.

He and Mardana were also taken prisoners and made to work. Guru Nanak began singing the holy songs to all the prisoners gathered around him, and their work wonderously began to be get done by itself. The commander, Mir Khan, was amazed and he quickly informed Babar about it. The conqueror soon came to see the supernatural phenomenon and heard the soothing songs sung by the holy man.

He asked, "Guruji, what is the meaning of the verses that you were singing?"

"I am requesting God to see how Babar had misused his power," replied Guru Nanak.

"God made you powerful and a leader so that you can use this power to help and protect your people rather than to hurt them," continued Guru Nanak.

Guru Nanak's words stirred deep into Babar's heart and he not only ordered the release of all the prisoners but also returned their properties.

Guru Nanak blessed Babar with a long rule in India with his descendants ruling over it. He also advised Babar to treat India as his own homeland as this would make his rule a long lasting and peaceful one.

Babar followed the Guru's advice and became a just ruler. Guru Nanak had succeeded in reforming one of the most terrible man on earth into a just and a wise ruler.

Back Home

After leaving Saidpur, the Guru went back to his home in Kartarpur. He stayed with his family for eight years. Here he proved that a man can serve both God and man, even as a householder; he showed people that one did not have to renounce the world to be a religious man. He even went against the conventional traditions by wearing ordinary clothes instead of the usual saffron dress. Guru Nanak did this to show to the world that once a man had given up his family life for a religious one, it did not mean he could not re-adopt his family life. He also wanted to show that truly righteous men were free to choose any kind of life or dress they liked, as long as they were true to the principles of their religions.

He gave his village people three golden rules to live by. First, that "A man should earn his living by honest labour."

Second, "He should always share whatever he has with those who are needy."

Third, "He should never forget God and see that no one else forgets Him either."

In his life, Guru Nanak practised what he preached. He worked in his fields as he used to do earlier and did all kinds of manual labour. He raised crops for his family and offered free kitchen or *langar* to all who needed food. In his *langar*, there was no discrimination among people. All lived and worked like a family with Guru Nanak as the head of the family. At the same time, he devoted himself to the work of God. His disciples named 'Sikhs' always gathered around him at Kartarpur, while he sang sacred hymns and talked to them about life and religion.

Bhai Budha

It was during his stay at Kartarpur, that Guru Nanak visited the nearby Amritsar district. There he met a boy who was grazing a herd of cattle. Guru Nanak saw in him the makings of a respected and devoted disciple. Guru Nanak called him, and asked him about his village and parents. Calling the boy over to him, he found that his name was Bura and he was a *Jat* living in Ramdas.

Bura was deeply influenced by the Guru. He found out the name of the village where he lived and next morning went to him with a pot full of milk and presented it to Nanak. He then started asking him questions about life and death and the ways of serving God.

"You are a small boy and such issues should not be of your concern," said Guru Nanak.

He told him to live in God and let God live in him. It was enough to make Bura his most devoted disciple.

He became Bhai Budha, and served the Guru in every possible way. Guru Nanak made him perform the sacred ceremony of applying the *tilak* on the forehead of five of his successors. He was made the first *Granthi* of the Golden Temple (Sri Darbar Sahib) at Amritsar. He taught *Gurmukhi* to Guru Hargobind.

It was during his stay at Kartarpur that Guru Nanak's companion, friend, disciple and *rabab*-player, Bhai Mardana, left for his heavenly abode in 1591 A.D. Guru Nanak had his body cremated and took on his son Shahzade to be his *rabab* player.

Rise of the Second Guru

His stay at Kartarpur, in the last part of his life, was important in more than one aspect. It was here that he found the second Guru of the Sikhs, whom the world knows as Guru Angad.

Guru Angad's real name was Baba Lehna. He was born on March 31 in 1504 A.D. He was the son of Pheru Mal, a trader at Ferozepur. Baba Lehna first heard of Guru Nanak from Bhai Jodha who always sang hymns of the Guru. His songs had melted his heart so much so that he decided to go to Kartarpur and meet the holy man. Guru Nanak invited him to live with them at Kartarpur. Baba Lehna arrived the very next day, and spent the entire night doing all odd jobs in complete acceptance, silence and devotion.

Guru Nanak, however, made all his disciples undertake a test and the most worthy of them was to be made his successor. And so one day he put on shabby clothes, took an open knife in his hand and went to the forest. His puzzled disciples followed him.

On the pathway to the woods they found silver coins on the way. Some of the men following him left after collecting them; a few others followed him further and found gold coins scattered on the way. They picked them up and rejoicing returned home.

Only two Sikhs besides Baba Lehna followed him still further. There they saw a funeral pyre with a dead body beside it. Guru Nanak asked his disciples to eat the corpse if they wished to accompany him. Those present flinched at the terrible idea and only Baba Lehna came forward, asking which part he should begin with. Guru Nanak was very pleased with Baba Lehna and blessed him saying that only he had understood and believed that he was an 'ang' of his Guru's body. He named Baba Lehna 'Guru Angad' from then on, since he had proved that he was a part and image of the Guru's own body. He was appointed the next Guru by Bhai Budha on June 4, 1539. Guru Nanak had bequeathed his seat to its rightful owner.

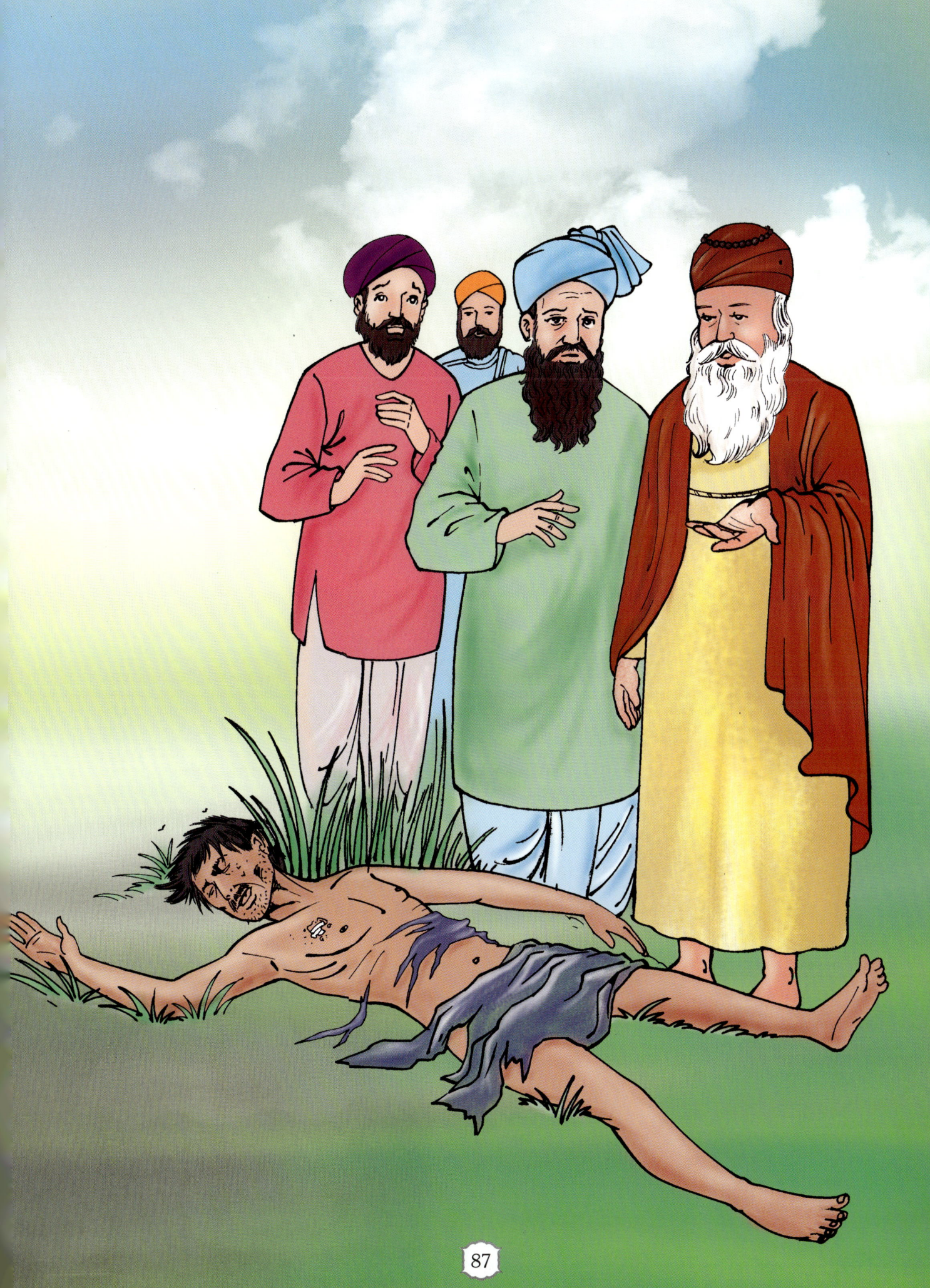

Attaining Samadhi

On September 22, 1539, Guru Nanak decided that his work as a mortal was complete after he had left a guiding light behind in the radiant person Guru Angad Devji. And so he left for his eternal home, back to the Supreme Being. He passed away at the age of seventy,

having fulfilled his mission in this world. When he breathed his last, his Hindu and Muslim disciples were engaged in a baffling dispute about the manner in which the last rites were to be performed.

The Hindus wanted their Guru's body to be cremated in the Hindu tradition. But the Muslims, who had been equally devoted to him and were his faithful followers, wanted a burial for him. A whole day passed and still they could not come to a mutual decision.

Next day, when they looked beneath the shroud, they could not believe their eyes! What they saw, to their astonishment, was that instead of the body, there was only a big mound of beautiful white flowers.

There was no doubt that it was the final message that Guru Nanak gave to his Hindu and Muslim disciples. It was a symbolic representation and message of harmony, peace and brotherhood of man that Guru Nanak had taught all his life. All the disciples present there hung their heads in shame at their ignorance and folly.

They decided to follow the Guru's advice and adopt it as a golden rule for life. They peacefully divided the flowers into halves, burying and cremating their share.

Guru Nanak, who had come into a world of disharmony, jealousy and eternal problems, left the world a better place than he found it. He had stayed among men for seventy years, five months and three days, teaching them to value life and love one another. He was the symbol of peace, love and brotherhood of man. He was a believer of humanity, and brotherhood, and his aim to cleanse the world of malice was fulfilled.

Glossary

Ang	part of the body
Avatar	Reincarnation
Batashas	little discs made of sugar
Bedi	a clan who are well versed in the Vedas
Brahmin	A person of the highest or sacerdotal caste among the Hindus
Brahm-bhoj	special feast
Chapati/roti	Indian bread
Dharamshala	refuge near a holy place
Fakir	a Muslim religious mendicant
Ghee	clarified butter
Granthi	the caretaker of a gurudwara and the reader of the Guru Granth Sahib
Gurumukhi	literally means "from the mouth of the guru"
Janampatri	birth chart
Janeu	sacred thread
Japji	set of verses composed by Guru Nanak
Jatt	an agricultural class mostly found in eastern and southern agricultural plains of Punjab and Haryana.
Jooti	handcrafted footwear
khadaun	wooden sandals
Khatri	a person who belongs to a Hindu mercantile caste alleged to originate with the Kshatriyas
Aayats	verse
Langar	kitchen

Madarsa	Islamic school
Mandi	market
Manjis	missionary centres
Maulvi	muslim teacher
Namaz	Muslim Prayer
Nawab	a person of wealth and prominence
Pandit	A Brahman scholar or learned man
Panja	five fingers of hand or hand itself
Patti	wooder tablet for writing
Patwari	an accountant
Pir	religious leader or prophet
Qalandars	A dervish who does not recognize outward mystical form or convention
Qazi	muslim judge who hears only religious cases
Rabab	musical instrument
Sadhu	an ascetic holy man.
Sahab	used formerly as a form of respectful address
Serai	place for the accommodation of travelers
Shastra	Sanskrit term used for scriptures
Shradh	a ritual to pacify departed souls
Tilak	saffron mark applied on the forehead as a symbol of auspiciousness in Hindu religion
Udasis	used for each of the four preaching tours of Guru Nanak
Yagnopavita	The sacred thread ceremony that invests the wearer with the sacred thread
Zamindar	landowner